IRISH   S

P A   T

Wl
Wh   ...velers bore us
With the praise of wine
While we have thee before us.

                    Joseph o' Leary.

Little Books of Ireland

First Published by
REAL IRELAND DESIGN LIMITED
27 Beechwood Close, Boghall Road, Bray Co.
Wicklow, Ireland.
Tel: (01) 2860799. Fax: (01) 2829962.
1993 1999

Design and Layout: Brian Murphy.
Photography © Liam Blake.

ISBN 0946887705

KENNEDY'S

VERY RARE

YEARS **7** OLD

IRISH WHISKEY

86 PROOF

PRODUCT OF IRELAND

IRISH DISTILLERS LIMITED

"ORIGINAL"

IRISH

THE VERY BEST

IMPORTED WHISKEY

BLENDED IRISH WHISKEY

BLENDED AND BOTTLED UNDER THE
SUPERVISION OF THE IRISH GOVERNMENT

THIS WHISKEY IS SEVEN YEARS OLD

100% IRISH WHISKIES

BLENDED AND BOTTLED BY
IRISH DISTILLERS LIMITED
DUBLIN, IRELAND

86.8 PROOF

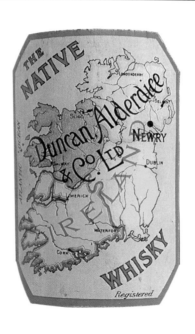

A SUPERIOR
BLENDED
IRISH WHISKY
PRODUCT OF IRELAND

100% IRISH

WHISKIES

4/5 QUART

86 PROOF

DISTILLED AND BLENDED BY

CORK DISTILLERIES CO., INC.

CORK, IRELAND

Austin Nichols
& Co. Inc.

NEW YORK
NEW YORK

53 Years Old IRISH WHISKEY
DISTILLED AND BONDED BY
George Roe & Co.
158 THOMAS STREET, DUBLIN
in the year 1919
GUARANTEED AND BOTTLED BY
DALYS, 10 EDEN QUAY, DUBLIN
70° PROOF $26\frac{2}{3}$ FL. OZS.

GREEN SPOT

IRISH WHISKEY

75cl ℮ 40% vol

MITCHELL & SON

Distilled, matured and bottled for
Mitchell & Son Limited, 21 Kildare Street, Dublin 2.
PRODUCT OF IRELAND

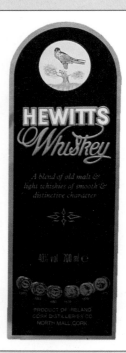

AGED **12** YEARS.

JAMESON

DISTILLERY RESERVE

IRISH WHISKEY

Matured in
Oak Casks for not less than
twelve years

40% vol.   PRODUCT OF IRELAND   700 ml ℮

DISTILLED, MATURED AND SPECIALLY BOTTLED BY JOHN JAMESON & SON, BOW ST., DUBLIN 7

DUNPHY'S

SPECIAL EXPORT

Blended Irish Whiskey

Distilled and bottled
by Irish Distillers Limited

40% vol.   700 ml e

Product of Ireland

Three Stills

IRISH SPIRITS

Distilled & bottled by
Irish Distillers Ltd.,
Bow Street Distillery
Smithfield Dublin 7.

PRODUCT OF IRELAND

30% vol.   Distributed by Fitzgerald & Co. Ltd.   700ml e

YEARS **12** OLD

REDBREAST

PURE POT STILL

IRISH WHISKEY

Matured in Oak Casks
for not less than twelve years

Fitzgerald & Co. Ltd.

Unique among whiskeys, Redbreast is a single, unblended, pure pot still Irish whiskey which has been triple distilled and matured in oak casks for not less than twelve years.

This uncompromising dedication to authenticity and quality gives Redbreast a traditional smooth mellow character and a taste which is full flavoured and assertive but not over robust.

40% vol.

DISTILLED MATURED AND BOTTLED IN BOND
FOR FITZGERALD & CO. 11-12 BOW STREET DUBLIN 7.

700 ml ℮

JOHN JAMESON & SON

CRESTED TEN

WHISKEY

by John Jameson & Son, Dublin.
Distillers of Fine Whiskey since 1780.

John Jameson & Son

Bow Street, Dublin 7

BOW STREET DISTILLERY DUBLIN

PRODUCT OF IRELAND

40 % vol.   700 ml ℮